Milepost 92½
Newton Harcourt
Leicestershire
LE8 9FH
Tel 0116 2592068

MILEPOST

The Golden Years of British Steam Trains

SR

SOUTHERN RAILWAY

MILEPOST

INTRODUCTION

The Southern, though by far the smallest of the Big Four companies, was a dynamic railway with some of Britain's best loved trains: The Bournemouth Belle, The Devon Belle, The Brighton Belle and The Atlantic Coast Express. The principal constituents were the London and South Western, South Eastern and Chatham and London Brighton and South Coast; and territory ranged from the Kent coast to Cornwall.

The company's commitment to extensive electrification meant that the development of steam traction was limited. The railway had far less freight than the other companies and served hardly any coalfields with locomotive coal having to be brought in from afar. The many pre-grouping designs inherited by the Southern were of great antiquity and contrasted with the prolific work of it's two principal Chief Mechanical Engineers, R.E.L. Maunsell and O.V.S. Bulleid. Maunsell's "Schools" were the most powerful British 4-4-0's and achieved legendary feats of haulage. The Southern was also distinctive in producing a revolutionary steam design during World War Two in the form of Bulleid's Pacifics which transformed the railway's express passenger services along with his Q1 Class 0-6-0s which brought to an end a 110 year long tradition of building inside cylinder 0-6-0s in Britain.

It is an interesting paradox that a railway so heavily electrified should retain so many antiquated steam designs and have the last main line to operate high speed steam expresses which survived on the London-Bournemouth and Weymouth route until 1967 – only one year before steam ended in Britain and almost twenty years after the Southern had ceased to exist. Some 1,845 Southern Railway locomotives embracing 90 different classes passed into British Railway's ownership in 1948.

A Wainwright Class C, 0-6-0 heads a down freight on Eynsford Viaduct.

Bulleid Merchant Navy Class 4-6-2 No. 35022 "Holland America Line" - in the short lived B.R. blue livery - spent some time in Rugby Testing Plant in December 1953/January 1954. No changes were made at the time, re-building commenced two years later.

Previous spread

The funeral train of Sir Winston Churchill on its way to Handborough (for Bladon and Blenheim) hauled by Battle of Britain Class 4-6-2 No. 34051 "Sir Winston Churchill" on 30th January 1965. The train consisted of Pullman Brake Car No.208, bogie luggage van No.S2464 (containing the coffin), Pulman Cars "Carina", "Lydia", "Perseus" and Pullman Brake Car "Isle of Thanet". Arthur Mace captures the solemnity of the occasion; the onlookers are not ordinary train spotters; there is an omnipresence about the characters which resembles a Munch painting.

Ashford based King Arthur Class 4-6-0 No.30802 "Sir Durnore" heads a local train to Ramsgate. Note the crossing keeper's cottage.

Schools Class 4-4-0 No.30918 "Hurstpierpoint" enters Ashford on a Charing Cross-Folkestone train, while a King Arthur Class 4-6-0 awaits the road with the Deal-Birkenhead train formed of W.R. stock.

It is Saturday and time to take the train to Canterbury for shopping and leisure pursuits. Class 2 MT, 2-6-2T No.41313 heads the train entering Aylsham.

Tunbridge Wells West with (left) an H Class 0-4-4T from Oxted, D1 Class 4-4-0 No.31470 approaching with a Tonbridge to Brighton train and an L Class 4-4-0 in the bay platform.

L Class 4-4-0 No.31769 approaches Orpington Station with a train for Dover via Ashford.

Passing Shortlands with a down continental express formed of the latest S.E.C.R. boat train stock about 1927 is King Arthur Class 4-6-0 No. E763 "Sir Bors de Ganis"

A chunky re-build of a Drummond 4-6-0, Class H15 No.E333 pauses at Axminster with a down Plymouth train.

Wainwright Class D, 4-4-0 No.1737 on a westbound train threads the white cliffs near the Warren Halt between Dover and Folkestone. The gentleman standing in the middle distance is presumably Arthur Mace's colleague and appears to have just photographed the train from a tripod.

Over page
Wainwright Class C, 0-6-0 No.31243 on shunting duties in the port of Dover. The ship is probably the "Isle of Thanet" of 1925, whose sister ship "Maid of Kent" was lost in World War Two.

King Arthur Class 4-6-0 No.30794 "Sir Ector de Maris" stands in the Night Ferry's traditional platform 2 at Victoria on a Kent Coast arrival.

Class I3, 4-4-2T No.2087 waits to depart from Victoria station on a Derby Day Pullman Race Special to Epsom Downs. In those pre-war days there would be several First Class race trains also steam hauled.

Another view of the former L.B.S.C. part of Victoria Station. A Brighton Works built L.M.R. Fairburn 2-6-4T has brought in an Oxted Line train forming the 3.8pm departure to East Grinstead.

During World War Two, with fears of possible invasion or aerial bombardment and a reduction in train services, many older engines were dispersed and placed in store away from depots. Possibly a unique photograph in view of the wartime veto on photography these three Stirling Class O1, 0-6-0's have been cleaned, their chimneys covered and fire irons removed. The two nearest, No's.1390 and 1093, were withdrawn in 1951.

Two Adams express locomotives of the mid 1890's await scrap at Eastleigh after the war. These 6' 6" 4-4-0s were T3 Class No.571 and X6 Class No.666. The former class is represented by No.563 in the National Railway Museum in York.

A line of withdrawn engines at Eastleigh in 1946. Leading is L.S.W.R. Jubilee Class A12, 0-4-2 No.555, L.B.S.C. Class D1 0-4-2T No. B633 and L.B.S.C. Class H1, 4-4-2 No.2040 "St Catherine's Point". They were towed away for scrap two years later.

Previous page
Wainwright Class E 4-4-0 No.31166 heads an up van train through Canterbury West. It was the last survivor of it's class being withdrawn in 1955.

Bulleid West Country Class Pacific No.34100 "Appledore" heads for London via Folkestone near Hawkesbury Street Junction. This once facinating area is now largely superseded by the Channel Tunnel. At right, behind the footbridge, the tracks lead into Dover Western Docks station recently closed.

Brighton-Cardiff through train near Lancing in the charge of West Country Class 4-6-2 No.34048 "Crediton" with G.W.R. carriages. The S.R. engine worked through to Salisbury.

The same location, West Country Class 4-6-2 No.34039 "Boscastle" heads the Brighton-Plymouth through train. Sets of pictures from the same location were a characteristic of Arthur Mace's work.

Drummond Greyhound Class T9, 4-4-0 No.310 pauses at Lewes with a Victoria-Eastbourne train prior to electrification in 1935. In S.R. days, several were fitted with six wheeled tenders to fit smaller turntables on ex-L.B.S.C.R. and S.E.C.R. lines.

A Brighton train enters Lewes from Eastbourne in the charge of an ex-L.B.S.C.R. Class B4, 4-4-0. Preparations for electrification in 1935 are in evidence.

It is blossom time in the Garden of England as Class D1 4-4-0 No.31735 heads a train over the S.E.R. route to the Kent coast via Ashford.

Previous page
A well known signal at the London end of Reading Station covering admittance to the former S.E.C.R. line at Reading South as well as the main line to Paddington.

King Arthur Class 4-6-0 No.30781 "Sir Aglovale" with an Ocean Liner express boat train from Victoria to Dover. Urie's L.S.W.R. Class N15 express passenger 4-6-0s with 6' 7" diameter wheels were incorporated into the King Arthur class by the S.R. More examples, with some modifications, appeared under Maunsell in 1925 and No 30781 is in this series. All examples had gone by 1962 but some of the names were inherited by the B.R. Standard 5 4-6-0s which partly superseded the King Arthurs, especially on the Waterloo, Bournemouth and Weymouth route so keeping the memory of these lovely engines alive until the end of S.R. steam in 1967.

Dramatic picture of an Ashford based Wainwright Class D, 4-4-0 on a Ramsgate-Victoria train. In pre-war days, a Pullman car was included on certain services on this route.

A busy scene at the Margate end of Ramsgate Station. Perhaps the coaling plant was out of order as engines are being coaled by crane on the right hand side. In the platform stands a Class D1 4-4-0 and at left a Class H 0-4-4T.

Between April and June 1948, two L.M.R. 2-6-4Ts, No's.42198/99, were loaned to the S.R. for trials, largely between Waterloo and Basingstoke and Victoria and Tunbridge Wells West. However, on 23rd and 24th April, No.42199 was tested between Victoria and Ashford via Maidstone East. It is seen leaving Ashford for London.

Two re-boilered Stirling Class R1, 0-6-0Ts, Nos.1337 and 1174, head an up continental express from Folkestone Harbour. A third 0-6-0T would be banking in the rear. At Folkestone Junction, a main line engine would take over. These elderly engines were replaced by surplus W.R. 0-6-0PTs in 1959 until electrification in 1961.

Battle of Britain Class 4-6-2 No.34066 "Spitfire" heads a down express on the Foord Viaduct at Folkestone. Beneath the viaduct is a Guy Arab IV of the East Kent Road Car Company.

Another view of the viaduct with a B.R. Class 5MT, 4-6-0 No.73087 on a down train.

An un-rebuilt Bulleid Battle of Britain Class 4-6-2 shuts off steam for a speed restriction while working a Victoria-Ramsgate train at Chestfield and Swalecliffe Halt, near Whitstable.

Re-built West Country Pacific No.34014 "Budleigh Salterton" on Foord Viaduct, Folkestone.

Again on the Foord Viaduct, Battle of Britain Class 4-6-2 No.34078 "222 Squadron". In the foreground is an East Kent Leyland PD1.

Stirling Class QI 0-4-4T No.A423 after its 1926 withdrawal was modified at Ashford Works for a stationary steam provision in which form it survived until 1933. This is surely one of Arthur Mace's most exciting pictures.

Previous spread
At Cannon Street, newly built Battle of Britain Class 4-6-2 No.21C167 "Tangmere" heads a down Dover express in the evening rush hour. This engine in un-rebuilt condition is undergoing restoration on the Mid Hants Railway.

The Erecting Shop at Eastleigh Works. Left and centre are two Class H15 4-6-0s, at right King Arthur Class 4-6-0 No.788 "Sir Urre of the Mount" still in wartime black livery.

Ashford Works Erecting Shop with Wainwright Class C, 0-6-0 No.1691.

A South Eastern and Chatham H Class 0-4-4T at Minster.

Canterbury West signal box with Classes H 0-4-4T and N 2-6-0 visible. The old Canterbury and Whitstable Railway engine shed can be seen in the background.

Class M7, 0-4-4T No.30047 heads a pull and push train to Brighton at Horsham Station, which was re-built in 1938 for the Mid-Sussex line electrification.

Schools Class No.30920 "Rugby" couples on to a boat train at Folkestone Junction.

South Eastern and Chatham Class D1, 4-4-0 No.31749 heads an up train at Sittingbourne Junction (for Sheerness).

The N Class Moguls were predominant in workings over the Reading-Redhill line. Here No.31411, one of the last batch to be built in 1933, heads a train through Gomshall and Shere.

Opposite
A Bulleid Battle of Britain Class Pacific nears the end of it's journey as it enters Birchington on Sea with a Victoria-Ramsgate express.

Previous spread
A D1 Class 4-4-0 with a lattice post London Chatham and Dover Railway signal.

Over page
A scene in the shed yard at Ramsgate with a Schools Class 4-4-0 taking coal. At right a Class H 0-4-4T and a Class T9 4-4-0 complete this pre-war view.

An interesting comparison of two railway's main line goods engines at Stewarts Lane shed Battersea. At left ex-S.E.C.R. Wainwright Class C, 0-6-0 No.31724 at right ex-L.B.S.C.R. Class C2x, 0-6-0 No. 32437. There was not a lot to choose between them but each railway's drivers preferred their own. In World War One, both companies introduced 2-6-0s for heavy freight work. Above, a King Arthur Class 4-6-0 heads a down express.

A party visit to Hither Green Shed with cameras focused on an N Class 2-6-0 as a C Class 0-6-0 simmers alongside.

Shed shunting in progress at Ramsgate Shed, with the engines in wartime black livery. At left re-boilered Stirling Class B1, 4-4-0 No.1452 (withdrawn in 1950), while a Class C, 0-6-0 shunts Class H, 0-4-4T No.1523. In the distance on the turntable stands a Class L1 4-4-0.

A pleasant scene on the S.E.R. main line in Kent with Ashford based King Arthur Class 4-6-0 No.30803 "Sir Harry le Fiselake".

Hard working re-built West Country Class 4-6-2 No.34034 "Honiton" passes Mitcheldever at speed with a down Ocean Liner Express to Southampton docks, the Pullman cars suggesting it was a Cunard working.

A Southern Railway rail built upper quadrant signal frames H Class 0-4-4T No.31519 propelling a pull and push train to Oxted.

Previous spread
Two Schools Class 4-4-0s run neck and neck between Hither Green and Grove Park. On the slow line No.900 "Eton" is working a Charing Cross-Dover train, while No.906 "Sherborne" heads a Cannon Street-Hastings Train on the fast line.

Over page
One of Bulleid's powerful wartime Austerity 0-6-0s of Class Q1, No.33004, shunts a covered wagon at the south end of Guildford Station.

An unidentified Drummond T9 Class 4-4-0 drifts down the 1 in 37 bank from Exeter Central to Exeter St David's on a Plymouth train.

Bulleid Battle of Britain Class 4-6-2 No.34084 "253 Squadron" heads a Victoria-Dover express past Minster Junction having taken the S.E.R. route via Ashford.

Opposite
Re-built Class D1, 4-4-0 No.31743 pauses at Canterbury East on a stopping train to Ramsgate via the S.E.R. route.

Two Southern Railways Schools Class 4-4-0s at Waterloo both on Portsmouth trains.

Schools Class 4-4-0 No.30928 'Stowe' is seen passing Paddock Wood with a Dover–Victoria express. The coal wagon and sidings for mixed freight eloquently remind us how the Railway provided an efficient co-ordinated transport system in those glorious pre-motorway days.